SECRET KEEPER GIRL
DIARY

by Dannah Gresh with Lexi Gresh and You!

Hope
BIBLEChurch
HOPE ACADEMY

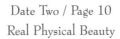

Hey, my name is Dannah, and this is my daughter Lexi. We like to paint our fingernails, eat Chinese, play with Lexi's hamsters, and shop till we drop!

We have a question for you: When you look in the mirror, are you more likely to say

Cool! Yeah, that's me!

 OR

Ewwww! Yuck, that's me?

I hope you picked letter a, but let's face it, you're a girl and you'll probably feel both ways sometimes, depending on which day it is. Beauty is a crazy subject when we mix it into how we feel.

Oh, but I don't want you to base it on how you feel. (That'll change a lot in the years ahead.) I want you to base your beauty on what God says. I believe in super fun learning. So, don't count on this Bible study to feel like homework. Secret Keeper Girl (SKG) is the most fun you'll ever have digging into God's Word. (Think: facials, tea parties, shopping challenges!)

Well, what are we waiting for?

Let's see what God says about your beauty!

(Dannah 6) ✳ Lexi

Your Beauty in God's Eyes

Welcome to SKG. That stands for Secret Keeper Girl, and I'm hoping you'll want to be one. What is a Secret Keeper Girl? Think hard and you may remember. Can you fill in this blank?

A Secret Keeper Girl is

. . . .

God Himself took time to carefully craft you into being! You must be a masterpiece!

> "We are the clay,
> you are the potter; we are all
> the work of your hand."
> Isaiah 64:8

girl gab!

Value Evaluation

OK, let's take girl talk to a new level. It's called Girl Gab. So, are you a Styrofoam cup, a ceramic mug, or a priceless piece of china in these areas? Look over the list and then write an "M" in the proper column for your mom and a "D" in the column that you think best reflects you as a daughter.

* Alyse

	Styrofoam	Ceramic	China
In the way I talk about my dad/husband			
In the way I talk to my mom/daughter			
In the clothes that I wear			
In the clothes I <u>want</u> to wear			
In the way I care for and style my hair			
In the way I care for my face each day			
In the way I care for my body and skin			
In the time I spend with God each day			
In the way I treat other people			
In the movies and TV I watch			
In the magazines I read			
The friends I select tend to be . . .			
My friends tend to pull me toward . . .			

Now for each area where you selected "Styrofoam" or "ceramic" for *yourself,* come up with one specific idea of how you can move toward presenting yourself as a priceless piece of china. For example, if you said that you are a Styrofoam cup "in the movies and TV I watch," you might write something like this: "I will try to limit my TV watching to thirty minutes a day and only watch shows I know to be clean and fun!"

Areas to Improve the Way I Present Myself

1. . . . .
. . . .
. . . .
. . . .

2. . . . .
. . . .
. . . .

3. . . . .
. . . .
. . . .

4. . . . .
. . . .
. . . .

5. . . . .
. . . .
. . . .
. . . .

A Tea Party!

DOODLE!

DOODLE!

DOODLE!

Tape photos here!

DOODLE!

DOODLE!

DOODLE!

This is what I thought!

Write down memories

Real Physical Beauty

So, can you find God's definition of beauty? Dig deep down under all this world's junk and you'll see it. It's nothing like what we imagined it might be. God's Word says this:

> "Sixty queens there may be, and eighty concubines, and virgins beyond number; but my dove, my perfect one, is unique."
>
> Song of Songs 6:8–9

Can you fill in this blank?
Real physical beauty is

. . . .

Real physical beauty is those special things about you that are unlike anyone else. Kind of funny, isn't it? Those are sometimes the things that make us feel most uncomfortable because they're . . . well, different. But God says that's what makes us beautiful. I want you to look at yourself piece by piece today. Can you see that unique beauty God created in just you?

girl gab!

My Unique Beauty

Complete the sentences below about yourself.
Take about ten minutes to do this.

My hair is. . . . .

My eyes are. . . . .

My nose is . . . .

My teeth are . . . .

My face is. . . . .

My complexion is . . . .

My smile is. . . . .

My weight is. . . . .

My height is. . . . .

My chest is . . . .

My legs are . . . .

My hands are. . . . .

My unique physical trait is

. . . .

. . . .

OK, let's be real! We all have things about us that make us feel more bashful than beautiful. What's yours?

. . . .

. . . .

. . . .

Guess what? God has got that covered! Second Corinthians 1:4 says, "Praise be to the God of all comfort who comforts us in all our troubles so we can comfort others!"

Some people might try to tell you that braces or zits are no big deal. But they are! Anything that makes you feel bad is a big deal. Just don't forget that God wants to comfort you, and it might just be to help the dozens of other friends around you who feel the exact same way about the exact same thing!

An area where I feel insecure about myself is

. . . .

. . . .

. . . .

. . . .

. . . .

Now, share your finished sentences with your mom.

Doodle Here!

Doodle Here!

Doodle Here!

Here's a photo of me getting a facial!

Diary Queen (that's me) says . . .

....
....
....
....
....
....
....
....
....
....
....
....
....
....
....
....
....
....
....
....
....
....

I think facials are really . . .

DOODLE!

DOODLE!

DOODLE!

Date 3

The Source of Beauty

Where does beauty really come from? As girls we sometimes get stuck thinking it comes from a great haircut or a totally awesome new fingernail polish. Sometimes we think it comes from being surrounded by beautiful friends or being noticed by cute guys. But these are dry streams. You won't find beauty there.

Can you fill in this blank?
The source of my beauty is

. . . .

"Your beauty should not come from outward adornment, such as braided hair and the wearing of gold jewelry and clothes. Instead, it should be that of your inner self, the unfading beauty of a gentle and quiet spirit which is of great worth in God's sight."

1 Peter 3:3–4

❋ Piakene

girl gab!

The Absolute Beauty Challenge

Let's go to the source, girls! I'd like to ask you to take my **A**bsolute **B**eauty **C**hallenge (A.B.C.). Here's how it works:

Challenge yourself each day to spend a little more time with God than you spend working on your external self. If it takes you about fifteen minutes to get ready each morning, set a goal of spending fifteen or twenty minutes a day with God. I want you to do this for the next four weeks, for five out of seven days a week. (We're giving you some days off!) To make it really fun and light, put something on the line in the event that you miss more than two days in a week. For example, if you miss you might say that you'll clean out your mom's shoe closet. She might agree to clean your hamster cage. It'll be fun to check up on each other that way! Something crazy and fun but not too awful! Keep it light.

Agree to the challenge by signing the Absolute Beauty Challenge. When you get home you can tape it to your bathroom mirror or somewhere in your bedroom where you'll see it every day.

Before you officially start your day, read the verse on the challenge and ask yourself the question, "Today, did I spend more time in God's Word or in front of this mirror?"

To make it easier, I've included twenty mini-devotions in the back of your diary. Why not try one now!

Absolute Beauty Challenge

(It's as easy as A.B.C.)

"Your beauty should not come from outward adornment,
such as braided hair and the wearing of gold jewelry
and clothes. Instead, it should be that of your inner self,
the unfading beauty of a gentle and quiet spirit
which is of great worth in God's sight."

1 Peter 3:3–4

"Today, did I spend more time in
God's Word or in front of this mirror?"

I, ... , will attempt to spend

. . . . .minutes a day in quiet prayer and Bible reading

during the next four weeks. I commit to doing this for

five out of every seven days. If I miss more than two days

in a week, I will . . . . for Mom.

Signed: . . . .

Date: . . . .

Quiet Solitude!

DOODLE!

DOODLE!

DOODLE!

Here are my favorite places of solitude

Secret Keeper GIRL

Write about how you sensed God in the
quiet of the place where your mom took you!

....
....
....
....
....
....
....
....
....
....
....
....
....
....
....
....
....
....
....
....
....
....
....
....

DOODLE!

DOODLE!

DOODLE!

Cool Stuff!

Date 4

The Power of Beauty

God created your beauty with a special power. The Bible calls it the power to intoxicate, but it's for just one man . . . your future husband. Each and every day the clothes you choose to wear are a part of saving the deepest secrets of your beauty for just him!

Can you fill in this blank.

The . . . . power of beauty
is

. . . .
. . . .

"May your fountain be blessed, and may you rejoice in <u>the</u> wife of your youth. A loving doe, a graceful deer. . . . May you ever be captivated by her love."
Proverbs 5:18–19

✻ Julianne

girl gab!

A Doodling Lesson

Check out this little graphic.
What do you see? Is he happy or sad? Hmmm!
I show you a couple of curved lines and a circle and you see a happy little guy! What is up with that? That's the Gestalt Theory in use. The Gestalt Theory teaches a designer to control a viewer's time by forcing the person to mentally complete a visual image. Because the brain is intrigued by completing the incomplete, it will always pause to finish an unfinished picture.

Check out this trio of circles.

What else do you see?

Can you draw a bird using the Gestalt Theory?
How about a mountain?

I'm not just telling you this for no reason. It has a lot to do with the power of your beauty. How? Well, what does a guy see when a girl walks by him wearing a tiny little pair of low-rider shorts and a belly shirt? Write your answer below:

How about when a girl wears a long, tight skirt with a slit all the way up the sides?

Are there any clothes that you wear that invite someone to finish the picture?

What can you do to avoid wearing clothes that invite people to finish the picture of your body?

25

DOODLE!

DOODLE!

DOODLE!

Tape photos here!

Artist genius in the making!

Secret Keeper GIRL

Here's everything we saw at the gallery!

....
....
....
....
....
....
....
....
....
....
....
....
....
....
....
....
....
....
....
....
....
....
....
....
....

You are God's masterpiece!

DOODLE!

DOODLE!

DOODLE!

Beauty is everywhere!

Truth or Bare Fashion

In the eighties when I was a teen, socks were huge! We had three pair of socks to match each outfit, and we wore them all at the same time! We even had something called leg warmers that were huge, fuzzy socks to wear over our jeans all the way up to our knees! Trends come. Trends go. Does God care about them? Fashion trends are not His biggest concern, but I think He does care. He certainly doesn't want us to just follow the crowd!

Can you fill in the blank?
I must express my beauty

. . . .

God's Word doesn't dis fashion. But it calls us to be careful in the way we express our beauty. If we obey Him, we'll probably stand out a little. That's a good thing.

> "Do everything without complaining or arguing, so that you may become blameless and pure, children of God without fault in a crooked and depraved generation, in which you shine like stars in the universe."
> Philippians 2:14–15

 *girl gab!*

Today's Hot Looks!

OK, let's test all the current fashion trends against God's Word. First, read all the different fashion trends I've listed in the left column. Go ahead and add any that you think I've missed. Include specific things you've had your eye on, like a certain style of shirt or a pair of sneakers. Now in the column labeled "How I See Them," write down the main characteristics or things people wear when they're trying to get that look.

Today's Hot Looks	How I See Them	Pass, Fail, or Use Caution
The Beach Look		
The Prom Look		
The Mini-Skirt		
The Cowgirl Look		
Grunge		
Goth		
Preppie		
Punk		
Athletic		
50's Look		
Designer Labels		
Belly Ring		
Tattoo		

This chart is from *Secret Keeper Girl* (Chicago: Moody, 2004), and may be reproduced as long as this permission line is included.

Now, let's look at a couple of verses and you can decide if these looks "Pass," "Fail," or deserve "Caution" based on a few Bible verses I think help us evaluate fashion. (Some of these will be familiar to you!)

Is this look feminine?

"A woman must not wear men's clothing, nor a man wear women's clothing, for the Lord your God detests anyone who does this."--Deuteronomy 22:5

God wants you to look like a girl . . . not a guy. That doesn't mean you can't wear pants. It just means you shouldn't wear pants that are cut for men or anything else that is considered manly in our society. Are there any things above that you feel God wouldn't want you to wear because they don't let you look like a girl?

Does this look hide my "intoxicating" secrets?

"Rejoice in the wife of your youth. A loving doe, a graceful deer. . . . May you ever be captivated by her love."
--Proverbs 5:18-19

God wants you to save the deepest secrets of your beauty . . . your breasts, your belly skin, your thighs, and your bottom . . . for just one man. Does this trend make you look fabulous without drawing attention to these parts of your body?

Is this look joyful?

"I also want women to dress modestly, with decency . . . with good deeds, appropriate for women who profess to worship God."
--1 Timothy 2:9-10

God wants you to look like a girl who worships Him. Since worshipping Him fills us with joy, we need to make sure that we don't clothe ourselves in dark and dreary attire. Are there any looks above that you should avoid for that reason?

Is it affordable?

"Your beauty should not come from outward adornment, such as braided hair and the wearing of gold jewelry and fine clothes. Instead, it should be that of your inner self, the unfading beauty of a gentle and quiet spirit, which is of great worth in God's sight."--1 Peter 3:3-4

God doesn't want you to be consumed with how much you spent on an outfit or whether it's a certain brand. It doesn't mean we can't have a certain brand if it's comfortable and affordable, but we can't whine for things we can't afford. Are there any things above that need to be disqualified for this reason?

Does it honor my parents?

"Honor your father and your mother, so that you may live long in the land."--Exodus 20:12

A Secret Keeper Girl can't wear anything her parents don't want her to wear, and she has to obey their preferences with honor. So, do you need to cross anything off for this reason?

Do I really like it, or do I just think my friends will like it?

"Am I now trying to win the approval of men, or of God? . . . If I were still trying to please men, I would not be a servant of Christ."--Galatians 1:10

It's OK to want something because you think it's neat, but watch out when you start buying things just because your friends have them.

Trends! Fashions!

DOODLE!

DOODLE!

DOODLE!

 Tape photos here!

This photo of my mom is worth some money!

You shine like stars in the universe!

Secret Keeper GiRL

Who invented the fashion trends of the eighties?

I mean, come on!

....

....

....

....

....

....

....

....

....

....

....

....

....

....

....

....

....

....

....

....

....

....

....

....

I'm a trendsetter with my heart!

DOODLE!
DOODLE!
DOODLE!

Be Yourself!

The Bod Squad

Well, here you are with your special friends, otherwise known as The Bod Squad! (Hi, friends!) I want you to offer each other positive peer pressure. Remember, peer pressure is when your friends or acquaintances influence you to do what is right or what is wrong. Do you remember what I said about peer pressure and fashion on the CD?

My . . . . of beauty is . . . .

. . . .

"He who walks
with the wise
grows wise."
Proverbs 13:20

OK, I'd just like to
update that verse for
today's SKG!
"She who shops with wise
friends will wear great
fashion!"

girl gab!

Truth or Bare Fashion Tests!

Before we set you loose to shop, I have a few modesty tests every single outfit has to pass. I like to call them the SKG Truth or Bare Fashion Tests. Review each test and take them as a group.

Test: "Raise & Praise"

Target Question: Am I showing too much belly?

Action: Stand straight up and pretend you are going for it in worship, and extend your arms in the air to God. Is this exposing a lot of belly? Bellies are very intoxicating, and we need to save that for our husband! **Remedy:** Go to the guys' department and buy a simple ribbed T-shirt to wear under your funky short T's or with your trendy low-riders. Layers are a great solution to belly shirts.

* Jessica

Test: "Grandpa's Mirror"

Target Question: How short is too short?

Action: Get in front of a full-length mirror. If you are in shorts, sit Indian style. If you are in a skirt, sit in a chair with your legs crossed. Now, what do you see in that mirror? OK, pretend it is your Grandpa! If you see undies, or lots of thigh, your shorts or skirt is too short. **Remedy:** Buy longer shorts and skirts!

* Tatum

Test: "I See London, I See France"

Target Question: Can you see my underpants?

Action: Bend over and touch your knees. Have a friend look right at your bottom. Can she see the outline of your underpants or the seams in them? How about the color of them? Can she see your actual underwear because your pants are so low that you're risking pulling a "plumber" exposure? If so, you bomb on this test. **Remedy:** Wear white panties with white clothes. If your pants are so tight that you can see the outline of your panties, try buying one size larger.

Test: Over & Out

Target Question: "Is my shirt too low?"
Action: Lean forward a little bit. Can you see too much chest skin or future cleavage? Your shirt is too low. **Remedy:** Today's fashions thrive on low shirts. Layering them is often the only remedy. Throw a little T-shirt under a rugby and you have a great look.

Too low, too short, too much, too tight, too small . . . test them all while at the mall!

Test: Spring Valley

Target Question: "Is my shirt too tight?

Action: Before I tell you how to take this test, I should tell you that you might not need it just yet. It all depends on whether God has chosen for you to begin to grow breasts or not. (And His timing is different for all of us, so be patient.) Maybe you can have your mom take this test! Ask her to place the tips of her fingers together and press into her shirt right in the "valley" between the breasts! Count to three and have her take her fingers away. If her shirt springs back like a small trampoline, it's too tight! **Remedy:** Don't buy clothes based on size. Buy them based on fit. Usually, you have to go a few sizes larger these days to have a modest fit.

Is My Swimsuit Modest?

Oh, girlfriend! That is a hard question. I would say that your swimsuit needs to pass nearly all of these tests. Can you raise and praise without showing off your belly? Can you bend over without showing off cleavage? Can you sit Indian style and look in a mirror without your suit gapping at the crotch? And still . . . swimsuits aren't high on the modesty scale unless you're in the water! So, when you jump out don't flaunt your body, cover up with one of the cute little cover ups available today or a simple pair of shorts and a T-shirt!

Fashion Testing!

DOODLE!

DOODLE!

DOODLE!

Me in my SKG challenge outfit!

Here is a doodle of me and my friends!

The Roarin' 20's swimsuit!

Secret Keeper GIRL

She who shops with wise friends will wear great fashion!

I shop with the Bod Squad!

DOODLE!

DOODLE!

DOODLE!

How short is too short?

Date 7

Internal Fashion

Ever meet a girl who just looked so cool but then she turned out to be a snob? Notice how her beauty fades? Of course, maybe you've met a girl who at first glance doesn't seem that beautiful, but the more you are around her the more fabulous she looks to you. That's internal beauty you're seeing. An SKG isn't complete without fashion for her heart.

Finish this sentence.
My beauty is ultimately determined by

. . . .

One of the kinds of "garments"
God wants us to wear is submission.

"For man did
not come from woman,
but woman from man;
neither was man created
for woman, but woman for
man. For this reason,
and because of the angels,
the woman ought to have
a sign of authority on
her head."

1 Corinthians 11:8–10

Women in Bible days were so committed to the internal fashion of submission that they wore their hair a certain way as an external reminder for themselves and everyone else around them. Wow!

girl gab!

Fashion For My Heart

Clothes aren't all that we wear. God invites us to "wear" things on the inside too. Check out these verses and discover some of the hottest fashions for the heart. **Underline the things we're called to "wear."**

"[A woman of God] is clothed with strength and dignity. . . --Proverbs 31:25

"Put on the full armor of God. . . . Stand firm then, with the belt of truth buckled around your waist, with the breastplate of righteousness in place, and with your feet fitted with the readiness that comes from the gospel of peace. In addition to all this, take up the shield of faith, with which you can extinguish all the flaming arrows of the evil one. Take the helmet of salvation and the sword of the Spirit, which is the word of God."--Ephesians 6:13-17

"I also want women to dress modestly, with decency . . . with good deeds, appropriate for women who profess to worship God."--1 Timothy 2:9-10

"Your beauty should not come from outward adornment . . . [but from] a gentle and quiet spirit . . . "--1 Peter 3:3-**4**

47

The things you've underlined are all vital parts of a SKG's wardrobe. But I think the most vital internal garment for an SKG is submission. Submission is allowing someone else to lead you. Submitting doesn't require you to mindlessly follow a bad example. Submission invites you to sometimes let a good friend get to play the game she wants to play even if you'd rather not. Submission requires you to quietly honor your parents, teachers, and other authorities with obedience. What a privilege! (What a tough task!) So, how do you know if you're wearing that? I mean, it's not like you can see it. Let's see if you've got submission hanging in your internal power wardrobe.

Submission Scale Quiz

Circle the statement that most sounds like you.

1 *When the kids I'm hangin' with decide they want to do something I don't want to do I:*
   a. yell and grumble and run home stomping all the way
   b. keep talking until I convince everyone to do what I want to do
   c. it's hard, but I try to listen to everyone's feelings and help us work it out
   d. do what my friends prefer; after all, everyone deserves a turn to lead

2 *When the teacher gives me homework, I usually*
   a. refuse to do it
   b. do it, but the whole time I think it's dumb because I already know it all
   c. wish I didn't have to, but I don't want to disappoint my teacher
   d. do it without thinking too much; after all, she's the teacher!

3 *When my parents ask me to do something I*
a. throw a royal fit and ask to be paid
b. grumble and do it half right
c. feel sad because I'm not getting to do what I want, but I get it done
d. do it with all my heart because I want to please my parents

4 *When one of my siblings wants the same video game or toy that I want I*
a. tease him or her the whole time as I play with the toy
b. tell him what I think he should be doing
c. ask if I can have it first and let the other person wait for his or her turn
d. let the other person go first as I find something else to do

5 *When I think someone has made a mistake I*
a. want to be the first to correct the person as loudly as possible
b. try to take over because I can do it better
c. watch for a good time to bring it up quietly
d. wait for adults or others in authority to make things right

6 *I go to church because*
a. my parents make me, but I wouldn't if I could help it
b. I have to, but I never really learn anything
c. I have good friends there
d. I want to be what God wants me to be, and church is a great place to learn

So, how'd ya do? Count up all your a's, b's, c's and d's. Write the totals below.

_____A _____B _____C _____D

Which letter did you have the most of? Circle that letter below to find out how you're doing.

Submissive Servant
Wow! I wish I could score this high. Keep up the great work. Just don't let it go to your head.

Sensitive Socialite
Good eye, girlfriend. You recognize your own desires, but you're trying so hard to put others ahead of yourself and you often succeed.

Boisterous Boss
Try harder! You probably have a lot of leadership potential, but God can't use that until you learn some gentleness. Work on controlling your tongue.

Raging Rebel
Uh oh! Watch out! You're wearing the wrong stuff, girl. You need to work on controlling your tongue and your emotions.

Hannah

Internal Beauty!

My Heart! Can't take a photo of it.

So here's a doodle of what it looks like!

DOODLE!

DOODLE!

DOODLE!

A woman of God is clothed with strength and dignity.

....
....
....
....
....
....
....
....
....
....
....
....
....
....
....
....
....
....
....
....
....
....
....
....
....
....

Keep up the great work!

DOODLE!
DOODLE!
DOODLE!

Here are photos from the beauty salon!

DOODLE!

DOODLE!

DOODLE!

Date 8

Affirmation of Beauty

Here we are! It's our last date.
(Oh, if I wasn't so excited I might cry!)

And I've saved the very best for last. It turns out you're not just beautiful, you're a princess. Imagine that? The God of the universe looking down and calling you a princess.

Here's your final truth.
God calls you a . . . . ,
and He is enthralled by your beauty!

> "The king is enthralled by your beauty; honor him, for he is your lord. . . . All glorious is the princess within her chamber."
> Psalm 45:11, 13

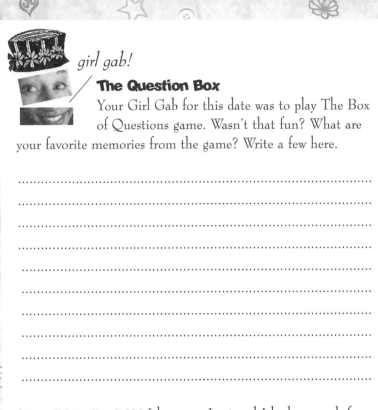

girl gab!

The Question Box

Your Girl Gab for this date was to play The Box of Questions game. Wasn't that fun? What are your favorite memories from the game? Write a few here.

....
....
....
....
....
....
....
....
....
....

Well, did ya like SKG? I hope so. Lexi and I had so much fun doing all the dates and getting all that girl talk in. It just fills ya up! But mostly, my sweet SKG, have you come closer to understanding your beauty in Christ? He is truly enthralled by your beauty. Stay super close to Jesus through devotions and you'll always have a little sense of that beauty. (Even on bad hair days!) But stray too far in this crazy world . . . well, just don't do that, OK!

I've had the next page designed just for you to write a thank you note to your mom for all the dates. Give her a hug from me, too!

XXX OOO
In Jesus' Great Love,
Dannah

Thank you for all the great dates!

You are a Princess!

tape
photos
here!

tape
photos
here!

tape
photos
here!

This is what our special date looked like!

Secret Keeper GIRL

The God of the universe is looking down and calling you a princess!

frills!

DOODLE!
DOODLE!
DOODLE!

Here are   more photos from our date!

DOODLE!

DOODLE!

DOODLE!

Candlelight and real linen!

dress up!

Secret Keeper GIRL

SKG Devotions

We're going to spend a lot of time together, my SKG! Cool! I've got some wild stories to tell you and some awesome truths. Each day during your SKG devotions, just read the Scripture and devotion of the day. Then, you get to write a prayer to God in your diary.

It'll be fun! Come on!

* Kelly

In the Morning I Lay My Requests Before You

"In the morning, O Lord, you hear my voice; in the morning I lay my requests before you and wait in expectation."
PSALM 5:3

I don't know about you, but I'm not much of a morning person. In fact, I can be downright grumpy. But seven years ago God showed me the verse above and others like it. *"In the morning, O LORD, you hear my voice; in the morning, I lay my requests before you and wait in expectation."* Was God really calling ME to get out of bed a few minutes earlier to talk to Him? I confessed to Him that I wasn't sure I could do it and I needed His gentle, loving help.

The most amazing thing happened the very next morning. My alarm went off to get me up to do my devotions and I really, really, really wanted to go back to sleep, but suddenly I heard a tapping at my back door. *Who could be tapping at my back door so early?* I thought. I dragged myself out of bed, only to find no one there. I crawled back into my warm, comfy bed only to have that tap-tap-tapping rudely call me to check the back door again. I got there and NO ONE was there. I went back into my room and waited, thinking someone must be playing a trick on me.

Soon, the tapping came back. I got down on all fours and snuck out under my dining room table. I was staring at my glass door where I saw the most amazing thing. A tiny bird was sitting on my deck tapping on the glass. HA! What a funny way for God to awaken me, I thought. How tender! How loving! How hilarious! That little bird came back every morning for the next three days, luring me out of bed. (One morning I even had Robby and Lexi sneak out with me to see him so people would actually believe me!) I believe that was God's big answer to me that He really does want my attention first thing in the morning. I confess it has been hard for me, but since that little bird visited my deck I've been giving my best effort to hear God's voice IN THE MORNING!

In Your Journal Today:
Rewrite Psalm 5:3 into your journal and write a prayer to God asking Him to help you to talk to Him "in the morning."

SKG Devotions

Day 2

Earnestly I Seek You
READ PSALM 63

"O God, You are my God, earnestly I seek You; my soul thirsts for You."
PSALM 63:1

I have a missionary friend named John who went to a Spanish-speaking country to help build a church. Most of the crew were not Christians, but John wanted to share God's love with them, so he built the church with them. They taught him some Spanish so they could communicate better. One day the missionary supervisor came to see how John was doing. He saw John ask for the hammer and the other guys giggled. He saw John ask for a saw and, again, the guys giggled. The missionary looked concerned. He pulled John to the side and asked him why he was calling the workers bad names when he asked for things. John looked over at the workers, who were howling with laughter. The joke was on John. He didn't know Spanish, and so he didn't know he was actually saying, "Pass the hammer, jerk!" or "Pass the saw, loser!"

Sometimes we have a translation difficulty with the Bible. You see, it wasn't actually written in English. It was written in Hebrew, Greek, and Aramaic. Translating the Bible into English from these very complicated languages was a big task, and so sometimes we get a very simplified version or a version that just doesn't say what God actually meant for us to know. That's why you must study diligently. Today's memory verse is a good example of what I'm talking about. Read the verse at the top of the page.

The word "earnestly" is actually the Hebrew word "scachar," which means "dawn, early, rising in immediate pursuit." In other words, talking to God should be the very first thing we do in the day. If your morning routine is so rushed that you can't spend time with God, try to get up a little earlier. If you're just "not a morning person" it's OK to have your quiet time with God later in the day, but be sure to utter a prayer to give Him your day as you awaken!

In Your Journal Today:

Rewrite Psalm 63:1 into your journal. Write about a day when you really felt "thirsty" for God. What did that feel like? Tell Him!

SKG Devotions

Day 3

Seek First the Kingdom of God

READ MATTHEW 6:25–34

"Seek first his kingdom and his righteousness,
and all these things will be given to you as well."
MATTHEW 6:33

When I was not much older than you, I felt like God wanted me to help a ministry teach children about Jesus. I wasn't old enough to actually be a teacher, so I volunteered to be a helper. That same summer a lot of my friends were going to the beach every day and planning a lot of cool things. I felt a little left out, but I kept believing that when I seek God's kingdom first, "all these things" would be given to me as well. For me at that age, "all these things" meant some fun and sun. That summer God blessed me amazingly with a scholarship to the most awesome Christian camp near Pittsburgh. I got to go caving, rock climbing, and horseback riding, and I tried my hand at archery, self-defense, candle-making, and all kinds of stuff. It was so amazing. God really does bless our socks off when we seek His kingdom first.

How do you think that God wants you to seek His kingdom? Is there a friend who isn't the most fun to be with but needs your love right now? Is there someone you need to pray for more?

What are "all these things" in your heart? They're different for all of us. Is it a happier home? Is it a better teacher? Is it more friends? Is it a certain thing you're hoping to do?

Guess what? God already knows about it, and so you might as well tell Him.

In Your Journal Today:

Rewrite Matthew 6:33 into your journal. Write a prayer asking God to show you how you can seek His kingdom and ask Him to help you to do that first rather than trying to get "all these things!" Trust Him to provide them or to change your heart.

SKG Devotions

Day 4

Behold I Stand at the Door and Knock
READ REVELATION 3:14–22

"Here I am! I stand at the door and knock. If anyone hears My voice and opens the door, I will come in and eat with him, and he with Me."
REVELATION 3:20

There is a story about a family who was in a flood and prayed for God to rescue them. Soon a boat floated by and a man offered to pick them up. The family said, "No, it's OK, we're waiting for God to rescue us!" After a while longer, a helicopter came by and dropped down a lifeline. The family refused it because they were waiting for God. Hello! Do you think that just maybe God had sent that boat and that helicopter?

Today's verse talks about God standing at the door and knocking. A lot of people use this verse to explain that Jesus is talking to unbelievers and saying He wants to be with them. But that's not an accurate use of this verse. Look at the heading just before verse 14. In my Bible it says, "To the CHURCH in Laodicea!" This verse is written to those who already believe that Jesus is their Savior. And it says, "Here I am! I stand at the door and knock . . . open the door!" Sometimes as believers we really need to slow down and realize that God needs us to respond to something He's already doing in our lives.

Is there something you've been praying about for a while? Is it possible that God has already sent a boat or a helicopter to say "Here I am"? Take a moment today to look around to see where God is knocking at the door of your life.

In Your Journal Today:
Rewrite Revelation 3:20 into your journal. Sit quietly before God today and just let Him reveal to you where maybe He's been knocking at the door of your life. After you do this, write about what God tells you.

SKG Devotions

Day 5

Look At Us!

READ ACTS 3:1–10

"Peter looked straight at him, as did John. Then Peter said, 'Look at us!'"
ACTS 3:4

Ever wonder about the term "born again"? In John 3, Jesus tells Nicodemus that he must be "born again." Nicodemus even asks, "How can an old man get back into his mother's belly?" (See verse 4.) But Jesus is talking about something symbolic, not literally being born again. What does it mean?

Well, pretend with me for a moment that you are a baby still stuck in your mother's warm, wet belly. You are fully developed and ready to be born. You can even hear the distant world outside your mother's belly. But what of that world can you see? Nothing, right? No brilliant colors. No sunshine. No rainbows. No smiling faces. No acts of love. You cannot see until you are born. Then suddenly the wonders of this world are fully exposed for you to see.

It's like that for people who don't know Jesus as their Lord and Savior. They just don't "get it" sometimes because they cannot "see" what you see in the spirit world. They can't see God's love. Can't see God's healing. Can't see the warmth of fellowship in a Bible study group. They haven't been born into that world yet.

What *can* they see? They can see you! Our Bible reading today tells about a man who needed physical healing. It's funny that Peter says, "Look at us!" Why didn't he say, "Look at God"? Two reasons. One, the man wasn't a believer yet, and so he was blind to God. But also because Peter and John were living so very much as God wanted them to, that they could confidently say "Look at us!" knowing that the man would see proof of God. Is your life like that? Can your friends who can't see God see proof of Him in your life?

In Your Journal Today:

Rewrite Acts 3:4 into your journal. In your journal, write a prayer of confession admitting what areas of your life need to better reflect God. Then, ask God to help you to be more like Him in that area so others can see God's power in your life.

SKG Devotions

Day 1

Seeing God in His Creation

"I lift up my eyes to the hills—where does my help come from? My help comes from the Lord, the Maker of heaven and earth."
PSALM 121:1–2

About seven years ago, I was sitting on the beach feeling very sad. I was sitting right where the foam and waves just touch the sand, making it smooth like cement when they subside back into the ocean. I was wondering if God even cared about me because I was so discouraged. So, I asked Him. "God, do You even care?" Suddenly my eye caught some movement on that smooth sand. I moved closer. This time when the waves came up I saw clearly that dozens upon dozens of teenie, tiny clams were being washed onto shore. A few seconds after the water subsided, they all suddenly stood on end like tiny little soldiers and wriggled their way down into the depths of the cool sand. I thought this was amazing that God created these teenie, tiny, insignificant creatures with a way to protect themselves from drying out in the hot sun. Suddenly, it hit me. If God cares about those little clams, of course He cares about me! It was like a big hug from God.

The Bible is full of God communicating to people He loves through His creation.

This week, we're going to look at some ways that God speaks to us through creation . . . and to Y-O-U! You might want to plan to have your devotions outside or near a window so you can be close to creation when you are talking to God.

In Your Journal Today:

Rewrite Psalm 121:1–2 into your journal and write a prayer to God asking Him to help you notice Him in creation this week. Maybe write about a time when you remember seeing God in creation.

SKG Devotions

Day 2

Burning off the Chaff

READ LUKE 3:15–18

"He will burn up the chaff with unquenchable fire."
LUKE 3:17B

In Australia there are great, horrible "bush" fires. (We might call them forest fires.) When I was visiting Australia, I sat in a restaurant overlooking a valley that had been entirely burned out. The flames had obviously come within feet of the restaurant. I asked my tour guide, "How do they fight the fire?" He replied, "We don't. It's too powerful, and its purpose is really to make the bush stronger, so it must burn." He went on to explain that the trees making up the bush had a cone so hard and so thick that the only thing that would allow the seed to pop out and begin to grow was intense heat. When the cones heated up, they burst and the bush could continue growing. The fire also burned off the weak, dry, and dying trees. So you see, the fire is really a good thing.

John the Baptist said something about fire when the people asked him if He was "the Christ." He said that Jesus would burn up the chaff (the useless, inedible stuff that's left after wheat is harvested—yuck!) with unquenchable fire. In other words, in your life and mine Jesus might sometimes let things get really hard and difficult for us. He does this to burn off the useless things in our lives (the chaff) and to let seeds of growth sprout in us.

Has your family ever been through a hard time? Have you ever wondered why God was allowing it? Wait until you see what God allows to grow in your life before you question what God was up to. It's usually something really good.

In Your Journal Today:

Rewrite Luke 3:17. In your journal, write a prayer to God asking Him to help you to endure the "fire" of something that is really hard for you right now. Tell God that you'll trust Him to make something good grow as He burns away the useless things in your life.

SKG Devotions

Day 3

Even a Donkey
READ NUMBERS 22:21–35

"The donkey saw me and turned away from me these three times.
If she had not turned away, I would certainly have killed you by now,
but I would have spared her."
NUMBERS 22:33

When was the last time you saw a donkey speak? (Maybe when you watched the movie *Shrek,* but hey . . . that's only a cartoon!) In the Bible God actually caused a donkey to talk. He used this little creature to both save and direct the man named Balaam. Balaam was going somewhere God didn't want him to go. God was allowing him to go as long as he only said what God wanted him to say. But Balaam struck out on his journey as if he was "the man." God sent an angel to get his attention, but only Balaam's donkey saw him. How many times? Three times! And then, the donkey talked! (Would you have thought you were losing your mind or what?)

My friend, God used a mere donkey. Is He not going to also mightily use you during the course of your life? Oh, He certainly is. Ephesians 4:7 says "He has given each of us a special gift according to the generosity of Christ." [NLT] Jesus has given you a special gift . . . or ability . . . that no one else quite has. (Kind of like giving the gift of speech to a donkey!) He's going to use you in a mighty, magnificent, and powerful way if you will let Him. After all, you are one of His most magnificent creations!

In Your Journal Today:

Rewrite Ephesians 4:7 into your journal. Write a prayer asking God to use you and to help you to see the special gift or ability that He has given to you. (It could take a long time to see it. I found my gift when I was twenty-six, but I had a hint about it when I was eight!)

SKG Devotions

*NOTE: It is best if you do this devotion outside during daylight
when you can do some bird watching!*

Soar on Wings Like Eagles
READ ISAIAH 40:26–31

*"Those who hope in the Lord will renew their strength.
They will soar on wings like eagles; they will run and not grow weary,
they will walk and not be faint."*
ISAIAH 40:31

Today is a good day to have your devotions outside if you can. If you can't, move to a window. I'm praying even now as I write this that the Lord will show you the most beautiful bird today. I'm praying that you'll be able to see one in flight. If you can, go outside and watch and wait for a bird to fly above you. Just sit quietly and think about God as you watch birds nearby. Imagine that this is the freedom with which God wants you to live every day. Let God speak to you.

SKG Devotions

Day 5

The Circle of the Earth
READ ISAIAH 40:21–22

"He sits enthroned above the circle of the earth."
ISAIAH 40:22

How do you know that this Bible you're reading is real and true and written by God? Think about it for a minute. It's a hard question to answer, isn't it? Oh my sweet friend, all of your life you will be searching for more and more proof that this Bible is real. And today I want to show you a secret treasure in the Bible that helps us to know that it is.

Read Isaiah 40:22 again. Where does it say that God sits? Above the circle of the earth, right? Wait a minute! This book was written when people still believed the earth was FLAT! How on earth did the writer know that the earth was a circle? (It would be years before anyone guessed that the earth was round, and when they did, people tried to kill them because it was so unbelievable to them!) This Bible verse can only be explained by one thing. The God of the universe who created the earth and knew it was a circle must have inspired the writer to say such a thing.

Astronaut John Glenn is a Christian. He says that he knew the moment he believed that Jesus was the Christ. It was when he was in outer space looking through a tiny window in his spacecraft back to the round, quiet earth. He thought of this Bible verse and suddenly realized, "God had to have inspired that truth!"

You can be certain that God is and that what He has inspired in the Bible is true to the highest degree.

In Your Journal Today:

Rewrite Isaiah 40:22 into your journal. In your journal, write a prayer of praise to God that is three sentences long. Use only things about creation to praise Him. Be creative!

SKG Devotions

Day 1

Praise God with Your Tongue!

"Whoever would love life and see good days must keep his tongue
from evil and his lips from deceitful speech."
1 PETER 3:10

OK, you may have already figured this out, but you're a girl! (What a concept!) As a girl you tend to talk a whole lot more than you would if you were a guy. Seriously, people have studied this. In one study, they watched pre-schoolers play. The boys? They were making all kinds of gross and loud noises. You can only imagine! The girls? Well, they were conversing as if they could fix all the problems in the world! In a study of adults they found that the average man speaks something like 10,000 words a day. Now that is a lot, but a woman speaks almost three times that many words. Talking is good, but God's Word tells us again and again that talking is something we have to be very careful with. So, we're going to spend all week talking to God about talking.

For today, I want you to praise God for the gift of speech. (Isn't it interesting that we praise God with talking?!) Go ahead! I want you to write a nice loooooong letter of praise to God. Just so you have an example, here's my praise about speech.

"Oh God, I thank You that You've given me the ability to speak. I praise You that I can tell my kids that I love them. I praise You that I can sing songs of worship. I'm thankful that I can giggle and tell jokes. God, let my lips always be a blessing to You!"

In Your Journal Today:

Rewrite 1 Peter 3:10 into your journal and write your
praise to God for your ability to speak.

SKG Devotions

Day 2

Taming the Tongue

READ JAMES 3:3–6

*"When we put bits into the mouths of horses to make them
obey us, we can turn the whole animal."*

JAMES 3:3

Once I was riding horseback with my friend in Missouri. It was all going along very nicely until we turned around to head home. The crazy animal couldn't wait to get there, I guess. It took off at lightning speed, and I was scared silly. I thought surely I would fall off, and so I tried to slow that beast with the bridle and reins. But nothing worked. Eventually I just held on and enjoyed the ride! I couldn't control the animal.

The Bible tells us that sometimes our tongues are like that. Uncontrollable. Girls sometimes struggle with this. I heard about two girls who showed up at youth group one night with almost the exact same new haircut. One girl squinted her eyes and said, "She's always trying to copy me. She did this on purpose." How silly. (And stupid.) But it was just enough to make the second girl feel really bad and use a few cruel words of her own.

Have you ever had a friend say cruel things to you? Do you remember how it made you feel? It hurts, doesn't it?

God wants you to control your mouth just like a bit controls a horse. Do you need to work on this area of your life?

In Your Journal Today:

Rewrite James 3:3 and then confess to God a time that your tongue was out of control and you said something unkind to someone. Ask God to forgive you and to help you be kind.

SKG Devotions

Day 3

Lying and Dying

READ PSALM 119:33–40

"Truthful lips endure forever,
but a lying tongue lasts only a moment."
PROVERBS 12:19

A few months ago I was asking God to show me if there were any lies in my life. I felt God telling me that I needed to be free of lying, but I just couldn't think why He was talking to me about this. I prayed that He would show me. The next day my mom brought out a beautiful clay pot that I had made in seventh grade. Only . . . I didn't make it. I always felt so good when I'd bring home a really neat art project and she praised it, so one day I brought home a piece of art that I did not make. Not only did I steal it, but I had lived with the lie of it for years. Soon I was confessing it to my mom and being set free from a lie told long ago.

Ya know, God doesn't like lying much. I think that's why old Ananias and Sapphira fell down dead . . . because they lied. Sometimes a lie can be big and bad like the one I told about the pot. Or sometimes it can be an exaggeration such as "I was on my best behavior in lunch today" when you really were a part of the group that got in trouble. Or a lie can be failing to speak up in truth, like when a teacher asks who did something bad in class and you just don't say anything even though you know. God doesn't mess with lying. He hates it.

But He loves truth. Is there an area in your life where you need to work on being more truthful?

In Your Journal Today:

Rewrite Proverbs 12:19 and then write to God about a time that you were not truthful. If it involves your parents, please go to them and confess it to them also.

SKG Devotions

Day 4

To Give Courage

READ 2 CORINTHIANS 7:13–14

Today's devotion is just a touch . . . a peek . . . into the apostle Paul's pride for his friends in Corinth. See how he uses words like "encourage" and "boasted" and "delighted"!

One day when I was a little down, Lexi snuck off and bought a special card and wrote me a note of encouragement. It changed my whole week!

God wants you to be an encourager. (*Encourage* means "to give courage.") For devotions today, I want you to write a nice note to a friend encouraging her for being a good Christian. Or, if the friend you're writing to isn't a Christian, thank her for being a good friend. Be specific about what you're thanking her for—what do you like about her?

In Your Journal Today:
No journal writing. Write a note and give it to a friend.

SKG Devotions

Day 5

Confession

*"Confess your sins to each other and pray for each other
so that you may be healed."*
JAMES 5:16

Sin makes us sick. Some kinds of sin make us physically sick, but all kinds of sin make us emotionally sick. Can you remember ever feeling really bad about something you did wrong? Well, today I want to share with you God's prescription for that sickness. James 5:16 tells us that when we confess our sins to each other, we are healed. Now don't be confused. Only God can forgive your sins, and don't let anyone tell you otherwise. You can confess your sins to God, and you must to be forgiven. But He has given us each other here on earth to help with the hurt. So, the healing for the sickness that sin causes comes from telling someone. (And that someone can help you not to do the same thing again.)

Secrets aren't a good thing when it comes to sin. I remember keeping a secret from my mom for years about a bad thing I did. I was so ashamed. I felt lonely and sad about it. Then, one day I managed to tell her about it and suddenly I felt great. My mom wasn't super mad like I thought she'd be. She was a little disappointed, but she helped me to figure out why I sinned like this and to make decisions so that I would not do it again. Don't let another day go by without telling your mom about anything you've done that needs to be confessed. You'll be glad you did.

In Your Journal Today:

Rewrite James 5:16. Today, write in your journal about something you need your mom's help with. Is it talking more kindly to your friends? Is it being more truthful? Confess this to her after you write about it, and watch to see how God will make your heart feel much better!

SKG Devotions

Day 1

Looking at the Heart

READ 1 SAMUEL 16:2–13

"Man looks at the outward appearance, but the Lord looks at the heart."
1 SAMUEL 16:7B

A homeless man in a tiny little town was accused of stealing a large basket of goods from a little grocery store. The police showed up at the grocery store with the homeless man and the stolen goods. The grocer showed much compassion. Rather than pressing charges for theft, he simply said, "Oh, I'm glad they brought you back! You left so quickly that you forgot your change." And he pulled out $38.12 and gave it to the homeless man and sent him on his way with the basket of goods.

Just a few days later the grocer was called to a lawyer's office. The lawyer explained that the homeless man had died and had willed all his earthly goods to the grocer. The lawyer handed the grocer a dingy, dirty bag. In that bag was some old bread, a Bible, and a bank book. The last deposit in the book was for $38.12, which brought the balance to just over $3 million.

The grocer's kindness was rewarded greatly, don't you think? The grocer did not look at the man's outward appearance, but he looked at his heart and his needs. And he showed much kindness.

In our Bible reading today, you see that God did the same thing when He selected David to be king of Israel. When Samuel went to find the future king, he was at first sure God must be talking about Jesse's oldest, strongest, wisest son. But He wasn't. He was sending Samuel to select David, who was Jesse's youngest, smallest son, and who still had much to learn.

Be kind to people. You may only see how they look today, but God sees their future and you might be an important part of it.

In Your Journal Today:

Rewrite 1 Samuel 16:7b. Write a letter to God about a person in your life who needs kindness but whose appearance is difficult for you to get past.

SKG Devotions

Day 2

A Wall of Faith

READ EPHESIANS 6:10–17

*"Take up the shield of faith, with which you can extinguish
all the flaming arrows of the evil one."*
EPHESIANS 6:16

In Bible days, there were a lot of terrible wars and battles. Each warrior had a shield to deflect the enemy's attack. The shield was thick and powerful and carefully crafted with ridges on the sides. When the attack was particularly difficult, the warriors would lock their shields together using the ridges and grooves to link them like puzzle pieces. They would then have an entire wall built in front of them to keep the enemy away.

Ephesians tells us that we need to have a shield of faith to protect ourselves from our enemy, Satan. It seems to me that, since the warriors linked themselves together with their shields, God used this analogy not only to tell us to be prepared to deflect the enemy's attack but to tell us to be prepared with friends and family members whose faith we can link into when the battle is heavy.

Which friends, family members, teachers, and church leaders do you spend time with? Are they believers whose faith is strong? If you were having a hard time, could you lock your shield of faith into theirs?

In Your Journal Today:

Rewrite Ephesians 6:16 into your journal. Write the
names of people who came to mind as you read
today's devotion . . . people around you whose
faith is strong. Thank God for them.

SKG Devotions

Day 3

Too Much TV?

PSALMS 119:33–37

"Turn my eyes away from worthless things;
preserve my life according to your word."

PSALM 119:37

My dad was the first kid on his block to have a television. (Think about it! I bet a lot of your grandparents never saw TV until they were your age! Strange, huh?) When I was your age, my dad had already logged a good twenty years on the tube, but one day he pulled quite a trick on me. He sat in his TV viewing chair and said, "Watch this! Today I learned how to magically change the TV channel." Then, he'd wave his fingers in the air and the channel would change. I was amazed. He did this again and again—turning the TV on and off and changing channels with a flick of his fingers. The joke was on me. I was the first kid on the block to have a remote control!

Today, the average kid your age watches three hours of television a day. (That's a lot of TV!) If they keep up at that rate, they'll see nearly eight thousand murders. Do you think that will affect them?

There are a lot of things in our world that can be considered "worthless things," and many of today's TV shows are among them. It can be hard to change your viewing habits if you're watching too much or the wrong kinds of things. You might try not watching any TV for a week. Or set a goal of only thirty minutes a day.

How are you doing? Are you filling your mind with worthless things, or are you allowing God to preserve your life with His Word?

In Your Journal Today:

Rewrite Psalm 119:37 and ask God to help you to monitor your television viewing habits.

SKG Devotions

Day 4

A Father's Love
READ LUKE 15:11–24

"For God so loved the world that He gave His only begotten Son, that whoever believes in Him will not perish but have everlasting life."
JOHN 3:16 (KJV)

There was a young man who'd grown up on an almond farm in California. He didn't want to be a farmer, so he asked his father for some money and left home. He left with a bad attitude. He found himself adventure in the form of a lot of sin. Eventually he realized how awful his life had become and how very much he missed his father. But he had become so worn out and broken. Of what use was he to his family now?

He sent his father a note. It said, "Father, I've sinned, and I want to come home. At 1:00 tomorrow I'll be on the train to come home, and it goes right past one corner of your tree orchard. Please cover one tree with a white sheet if I am welcomed. If I don't see it, I'll just stay on the train. Your humble son."

The next day, as the train neared the property, the son began to weep. He was so distraught he couldn't get himself to look. So, he asked an old man sitting nearby, "Sir, in a moment we're going to round a bend and you'll see the most beautiful orchard imaginable. Could you please look to see if one of those trees is covered in a white sheet?" The kind old man agreed to look. In a few moments the old man said, "Son, I think you need to see this for yourself." As far as the eye could see, every tree was covered with a sheet.

That's how very much God our Father loves you, my friend. There is NOTHING you can ever do to make Him love you less. While He does not desire for you to know the pain of living a life without Him and filled with sin, He's always ready to welcome you back.

In Your Journal Today:

Is there any area of your life that you need to give back to Him? A friendship? Your relationship with your parents? Bad music or too much TV? Write about that today in your journal.